Kindly Leave the Stage

A Play in Two Acts

by John Chapman

A SAMUEL FRENCH ACTING EDITION

SAMUEL FRENCH

FOUNDED 1830

New York Hollywood London Toronto

SAMUELFRENCH.COM

ISBN 978-0-573-69364-9   Printed in U.S.A.   #13611

IMPORTANT BILLING AND CREDIT REQUIREMENTS

All producers of KINDLY LEAVE THE STAGE *must* give credit to the Author of the Play in all programs distributed in connection with performances of the Play and in all instances in which the title of the Play appears for purposes of advertising, publicizing or otherwise exploiting the Play and/or a production. The name of the Author *must* also appear on a separate line, on which no other name appears, immediately following the title, and *must* appear in size of type not less than fifty percent the size of the title type.

CHARACTERS

CHARLES
MADGE
SARAH
RUPERT
MRS. CULLEN
ANGELA
NURSE
EDWARD

TIME & PLACE

The play is set in the living room of an expensively appointed garden flat in Hampstead.

ACT I

Evening.

ACT II

The same, fifteen minutes later.

ACT I

Scene 1

The sitting room of an expensively appointed garden flat in Hampstead. It has an alcove for the dining area. It is EVENING and as the CURTAIN RISES a couple are seen seated at the table, CHARLES and MADGE.

The table is set for four people. CHARLES and MADGE are in their early forties and well dressed. THEY are eating dessert and look somewhat ill at ease. There is a pause before Charles speaks.

CHARLES. What d'you think?
MADGE. It's awful.
CHARLES. I mean the pudding.
MADGE. Oh, I really hadn't noticed—not bad.

(Another pause.)

CHARLES. Needs a bit more sugar perhaps.
MADGE. Mm?
CHARLES. A little on the tart side, isn't it?
MADGE. Does it matter?
CHARLES. No, I suppose not.
MADGE. I think we should just get up and go.
CHARLES. Bit rude don't you think?

MADGE. It's not exactly the height of good manners for the host and hostess to have a blinding row in front of their friends and storm out of the room.

CHARLES. Perhaps there'll be a reconciliation.

(There is the sound of some PLATES CRASHING in the kitchen followed by a WOMAN'S MUFFLED CURSE.)

MADGE. I wouldn't bank on it.

(SARAH enters from the kitchen with a tray of coffee and puts it on the table. SHE is elegant and in her mid-thirties and in a violent temper which is held in check.)

SARAH. There's some cheese on the side there.

CHARLES. Thanks

MADGE. Sarah darling, coffee really isn't necessary.

SARAH. Of course it's necessary. Have you ever had dinner without coffee before?

MADGE. I don't know—I suppose I must—

SARAH. In my house?

MADGE. No no, not here of course.

SARAH. There's no need for an exception to the rule tonight.

CHARLES. I think, Madge felt that the sooner we were off the better.

SARAH. She needn't. We invited you to dinner and until you've reached the brandy and cigars you shall stay.

MADGE. I shan't want either darling.

SARAH. Charles enjoys them, don't you?

CHARLES. Normally perhaps. But under the present—er—circumstances, I think I could do without.

SARAH. Well don't, not on my account. Have you finished with the apple amber?

MADGE. It was delicious, Sarah.

(SARAH picks it up and exits to kitchen.)

CHARLES. Not quite as good as yours, darling.

MADGE. I shouldn't mention the fact.

CHARLES. 'Course not.

(RUPERT enters from the hall with a large steamer trunk.)

RUPERT. God, are you still here?

CHARLES. Sorry, old man.

RUPERT. No, it's all right. Just as well really. Excuse me, I've got a little tidying up to do. You'll be able to calm her down a bit when I've gone. *(HE goes to the writing desk.)*

CHARLES. She seems reasonably calm at the moment.

RUPERT. Before the next storm.

MADGE. I can't tell you how sorry we are, Rupert —

RUPERT. Oh can't you?

CHARLES. And if there's anything we can do—

RUPERT. Well there isn't, is there? We've run aground—hit the rocks. It's a total wreck, there's nothing to salvage.

CHARLES. I'm not sure what sparked the whole thing off. I mean, there we were thoroughly enjoying the pork en croute and the next minute the balloon had gone up.

RUPERT. (*Putting papers in his brief case.*) We got married, that's what started it.

MADGE. But that was twenty years ago.

RUPERT. And that outburst tonight has finished it. My only regret is that two of our dearest friends should have been here to witness it. But one can't legislate for the volcanic eruptions of life.

SARAH. (*Enters.*) I'm stacking the machine so if— (*Stops on seeing Rupert.*) For Christ's sake, don't tell me you're staying.

RUPERT. I wouldn't stay if I had two broken legs and a heart attack.

SARAH. What are you doing, writing me a farewell note?

RUPERT. I'm just getting some of my personal effects if you've no objection.

SARAH. (*Sees the trunk.*) We're dividing the property already are we? What are you taking, the sofa?

RUPERT. Credit cards, check books, that's all.

SARAH. Not the joint one?

RUPERT. (*Holding it.*) Well—I can't see that it makes much difference.

SARAH. Put the bloody thing back

RUPERT. All right, all right.

SARAH. You see what he's like? Devious.

RUPERT. The account's empty anyway.

SARAH. And mean.

RUPERT. Who spent it all?

SARAH. In case you've been away, some shops now make a small charge for food, wine, brandy, cigars—

RUPERT. Oh that rapier wit. In future all communication will be carried on through my solicitor.

CHARLES. Just a minute, that's me.

RUPERT. Oh God—so it is.

MADGE. That'll make things awfully awkward. Why don't you just separate?

SARAH. We don't want to separate.

RUPERT. No, it's got to be divorce for the sake of the children.

CHARLES. You haven't got any children.

RUPERT. Not by Sarah, but with my next wife the place'll be crawling with them.

SARAH. Someone in mind, have you?

RUPERT. Plenty.

SARAH. Oh, it's a harem is it? Now look Charles, you're our solicitor, not his, so you can represent me, O.K.?

CHARLES. Well—

RUPERT. Balls. Charles was my friend long before you came on the scene. We were up at Oxford together. It's been a lifelong association. Added to which, he's in full possession of all the facts, so it won't cost a fortune in research and endless letters.

SARAH. There you are, that's it, that's all he thinks of, money. Money, money.

RUPERT. It won't be too far from your mind when you're trying to live on your allowance.

SARAH. I doubt if I shall notice the difference.

MADGE. Actually, Charles's not a specialist in divorce.

CHARLES. More conveyancing really.

SARAH. Then convey him out of my life. Who wants coffee?

RUPERT. I wouldn't mind some.

SARAH. You haven't time. Now when would you like me to come to your office tomorrow? (*SHE pours three cups out.*)

CHARLES. I've got a string of meetings, Sarah.

RUPERT. And one of them will be with me. Shall we say ten-thirty?

CHARLES. Not possible I'm afraid.

MADGE. Then may I suggest you come to me.

RUPERT. I beg your pardon?

MADGE. I'm still a member of the legal profession.

SARAH. You haven't practiced for years.

MADGE. I only stopped for the childrens' sake. I'd enjoy starting up again.

CHARLES. Don't you think we ought to discuss it first, darling?

MADGE. We are doing.

RUPERT. Quite honestly, Madge, I'd prefer to deal with Charles.

SARAH. He's already booked.

RUPERT. Will you shut up?

SARAH. You see what a boor he is? He always shouts if he doesn't get his own way.

RUPERT. If I say I'm having Charles, then I'm bloody well having him.

CHARLES. Not unless I agree.

RUPERT. Why the hell shouldn't you?

CHARLES. Because you're over-bearing, conceited, and always have been. And the way you flew at Sarah during dinner—I'm surprised she didn't pour the gravy over you.

SARAH. Hear hear!!

RUPERT. I think you've had too much to drink.

CHARLES. I haven't had any since you charged out of the room.

SARAH. Have a brandy, dear.

CHARLES. Thank you, I will.

(SARAH pours one out.)

RUPERT. Hang on, that's mine!

SARAH. Only half of it—so he's having some of mine.

RUPERT. You can see, Madge, how extremely irritating she can be, I shall go and make some coffee. (*HE goes towards the kitchen door.*)

SARAH. You're sure you can remember how?

RUPERT. Did you get that Madge? If you hang around for another half hour, you ought to be able to compile quite a dossier on mental cruelty. (*RUPERT exits.*)

CHARLES. Frankly, I think we ought to be going.

SARAH. Before Rupert does? Don't be stupid. If you're not here he might attack me.

CHARLES. Has he done so before?

MADGE. I don't think we should discuss things like that. The case hasn't officially opened yet.

CHARLES. It's a perfectly reasonable question.

MADGE. My client isn't here to defend himself.

SARAH. Your client is a raving idiot with a very nasty temper. And the sooner he packs his bag and leaves, the better.

RUPERT. (*Opens the kitchen door.*) Where do we keep the bloody coffee?

SARAH. Next to the bloody tea, you helpless cretin.

RUPERT. Thank you, but it's a bit late in the day for compliments.

(SARAH picks up a cup and hurls it at Rupert and misses.)

MADGE. Heavens, are you all right?
RUPERT. Yes, she quite often misses.

(SARAH picks up another cup.)

CHARLES. *(Restraining her.)* Sarah please, you're not helping matters.

(The front DOOR BELL rings.)

SARAH. Oh God.
RUPERT. Who the hell—
CHARLES. Are you expecting anyone?
RUPERT. No. And we're not seeing anyone either.
SARAH. Madge—you go.
MADGE. Right.
SARAH. And whoever it is, get rid of them.

(MADGE exits.)

RUPERT. Probably the Vicar—collecting for a jumble sale.
SARAH. Perhaps he'll take a discarded husband.
RUPERT. Don't bottle it up, let it all come out.
CHARLES. Behave yourselves.

(MADGE enters.)

SARAH. Who was it?

MADGE. It was—and is—your mother.

SARAH. What?

(MRS DOROTHY CULLEN enters. SHE is smartly dressed and in her late sixties.)

MRS. C. Darlings, do forgive me. It's rather late in the day to be calling but I was driving in from the country and the car started making some very odd noises, so I thought I'd stop off here and let Rupert have a look at it. Don't let me break up your dinner party.

CHARLES. You haven't Mrs. Cullen, we were about to leave anyway.

SARAH. What are you doing in London?

MRS. C. Your father's having a few days golfing so I thought I'd stay in town and see some friends and possibly a show. You know what it's like trying to drag your father to the theatre.

MADGE. You're still enjoying life in the country?

MRS. C. Very much—yes. My husband never liked London. He hasn't set foot in the City since he retired, but he's perfectly happy for me to gallivant whenever I feel like it. So it makes for a very peaceful existence. How are the children?

MADGE. Fine thanks.

MRS. C. Final exams by now, I suppose.

MADGE. Mercifully we're through them now.

MRS. C. Oh, we're all getting so old.

CHARLES. I'm bound to say in your case—it doesn't seem to show.

MRS. C. How very gallant. Rupert dear, you haven't said a word since I arrived.

RUPERT. I'm sorry—it's very nice to see you again—you're looking terribly well.

MRS. C. Is that it?

RUPERT. Yes.

MRS. C. Ah. And what about you, Sarah.

SARAH. I'm all right.

MRS. C. You're looking peaky.

SARAH. Probably because I'm feeling "peaky."

MRS. C. I think both of you could do with a holiday.

RUPERT. I'm sure we'll both have one.

MRS. C. Where?

SARAH and RUPERT. (*Together*.) Italy/France.

MRS. C. Where?

CHARLES. Sort of on the border I believe.

MRS. C. I see. Now what about my car, Rupert?

RUPERT. Oh yes.

CHARLES. I'll have a look at it Mrs. Cullen. Rupert doesn't know one end from the other.

MRS. C. Rather like me.

CHARLES. Where are the keys?

MRS. C. In the dashboard, where they always are.

CHARLES. But you might lose the car doing that.

MRS. C. Well, at least I never lose the keys.

(CHARLES exits.)

SARAH. Have you eaten, Mother?

MRS. C. Yes—but I wouldn't say no to a cup of coffee.

RUPERT. I'll see if we've any cups left. (*RUPERT exits to the kitchen.*)

MRS. C. Have I upset him?

SARAH. No, Mother—that's his normal behaviour.

MADGE. Where will you stay in London?

MRS. C. I generally go to a small hotel just off Kensington Gore. Quite cheap and reasonably cheerful.

SARAH. How's Dad's lumbago?

MRS. C. Much the same—he can push a golf trolley round eighteen holes, but hand him the hoover, and he's locked solid.

SARAH. You shouldn't let him get away with it.

MRS. C. He doesn't. It's a very fair arrangement, he dislikes housework and I loathe golf.

RUPERT. (*Enters with a cup and saucer. To Mrs. Cullen:*) How d'you want it? Black? White? Sugar?

MRS. C. Just a little cream and no sugar.

MADGE. If you're not too busy you must come and have dinner with us one evening.

MRS. C. How very kind, I'd like that. And perhaps we could all have a meal at my hotel sometime.

RUPERT. We may be rather tied up for the next few days.

CHARLES. (*Enters.*) I'm afraid it's your big end Mrs. Cullen.

MRS. C. I beg your pardon?

CHARLES. It's gone.

MRS. C. You mean stolen?

CHARLES. No. The engine's broken. You can't possibly drive it.

MRS. C. You don't mean it.

CHARLES. I'm afraid so. You could wreck the entire car.

MRS. C. Perhaps I should get a cab then.

SARAH. I think you better stay here in the spare room.

RUPERT. I shall be in the spare room.

SARAH. You'd better not be.

MRS. C. Have you got a knife, Sarah?

SARAH. Knife? Why?

MRS. C. To see if I can cut the atmosphere.

SARAH. OK. We have some big news. And you're the first in the family to hear it.

MRS. C. God, you're not going to have a baby?

SARAH. No: a divorce.

MRS. C. Well—at your age, that's probably a lot safer. I take it Madge and Charles know?

SARAH. Yes.

MADGE. They decided this evening. It was all rather sudden.

MRS. C. It must have been.

CHARLES. Madge and I are handling the case.

MRS. C. Makes it rather expensive having two solicitors surely?

SARAH. Charles is representing me.

MADGE. And I'm doing the same for Rupert.

MRS. C. How cosy.

RUPERT. Would you like a drink, Dorothy—brandy or something?

MRS. C. If we're all staying up I may as well.

SARAH. You're behaving as though we're all having a jolly evening.

MRS. C. What do you expect me to do? Throw myself on the sofa and weep?

SARAH. You don't seem in the least surprised that Rupert and I are breaking up.

MRS. C. It's the pattern today—you hear of nothing else, and frankly I can't imagine why it hasn't happened before.

MADGE. You've seen the signs have you?

MRS. C. Madge dear, you don't need signs when two utterly impossible people try to live together.

SARAH. Since when have I been impossible?

MRS. C. Once you turned fifteen—you became rebellious, egotistical and your father let you wrap him round your little finger.

SARAH. Absolutely untrue.

MRS. C. You treated him like a door-mat. You alienate people.

SARAH. Rubbish.

MRS. C. He loved you Sarah. Just as once Rupert loved you.

RUPERT. And too she me.

(There is a pause. RUPERT has another stab at the line.)

RUPERT. Too, and she me. *(Another pause. RUPERT tries again.)* Me, she and too.

(Another pause.)

PROMPTER. *(Off.)* And she me too.

RUPERT. Don't quibble.

CHARLES. Rupert.

RUPERT. I'm sorry.

*(The CAST realize RUPERT is "lost" and try to put the
    play back on the lines again.)*

SARAH. *(Going back a few lines.)* Since when have I
been impossible?

MRS. C. *(Totally thrown.)* Pardon?

SARAH. Since when have I been impossible? *(Tries to
give Mrs. C. the line.)* Once I turned fifteen?

MRS. C. *(Grabs at it.)* Ah—yes. Once you turned
fifteen, you became rebellious, egotistical and your father
let him wrap you round his little finger.

SARAH. Absolutely untrue.

RUPERT. And absolutely wrong.

MRS. C. I mean your father let you wrap him round
his little finger.

MADGE. *(Helpfully.)* Your little finger.

MRS. C. Oh very well, "my" little finger.

SARAH. *(To the rescue.)* You mean my little finger.

MRS. C. Do I?

SARAH. Yes.

MRS. C. That's right of course, *your* little finger.

SARAH. Absolutely untrue.

MRS. C. You treated him like a door-mat. You alienate
people.

SARAH. Rubbish.

MRS C. He loved you Sarah. Just as once Rupert loved
you.

RUPERT. And too she me.

*(The play stops as before. ALL EYES are riveted on
    Rupert. He has yet another go at it.)*

RUPERT. Me she, and too.

(Another pause, then the PROMPTER is heard.)

PROMPTER. *(Off.)* And she me too.
RUPERT. Shut up!!
CHARLES. *(Quietly.)* Oh God.
RUPERT. What are you "Oh Godding" about?
CHARLES. *(Stage whisper.)* Pull yourself together.
RUPERT. D'you know what I'm going to do when the show's over?
CHARLES. *(Lost.)* No.
RUPERT. Kill you.

(The CAST now realize RUPERT's having a mental aberration and try to improvise.)

CHARLES. Perhaps we ought to go, Madge.
MADGE. Yes all right, Charles.
SARAH. *(Desperately.)* I'd rather you didn't.
MRS. C. *(Equally anxious.)* No, no please stay. I haven't seen you for such a long time. *(Groping.)* We must have so much to say to each other.
MADGE. *(Flatly.)* Yes.
MRS. C. Yes.
MADGE. Er—er—
MRS. C. *(Grabbing onto a previous line.)* How—er—how are the children?
MADGE. Fine thanks.
MRS. C. "O"s' and "A"s' by now I suppose.
MADGE. Mercifully we're through them now.
MRS. C. Oh, we're all getting so old.

CHARLES. I'm bound to say in your case it doesn't show.

MRS. C. How very gallant.

RUPERT. (*To Charles.*) Nasty little crawler.

MRS. C. (*Thrown for a second.*) Er—Rupert dear, you haven't said a word since I arrived.

RUPERT. Then you must be bloody deaf. I've said I'm going to kill this creep.

(Panic seizes EVERYONE again.)

SARAH. Er—

MRS. C. Er—

CHARLES. Er—

PROMPTER. (*Off.*) And she me too.

RUPERT. If you say that again, I'll shove the prompt copy down your throat!

MRS. C. I think I've chosen a bad night.

CHARLES. I think we all have. (*To the prompter.*) Bring the curtain down.

PROMPTER. (*Off.*) I can't.

SARAH. Press the button.

PROMPTER. (*Off.*) I've tried, but there's another twenty minutes to the Interval and there's no one there. They're all next door in the pub.

CHARLES. Wish I was.

RUPERT. I'll bet you do, Charley boy.

CHARLES. (*Trying to ignore Rupert and get back to the play.*) Er—Madge and I are handling the case Mrs. Cullen.

MRS. C. Yes, you told me.

CHARLES. Oh did I? Er—yes—well—

PROMPTER. (*Off.*) "Your daughter's finally decided—"

CHARLES. (*Cutting in.*) Your daughter's finally decided to slip her chains and run free.

MRS. C. Is it a mutual decision?

SARAH. Absolutely.

RUPERT. Completely.

MRS. C. Then why aren't you looking more cheerful?

CHARLES. I think what we're all feeling at the moment is shock.

SARAH. In my case it's anger.

MRS. C. You mean Rupert's been unfaithful?

SARAH. I doubt it, I can't imagine any woman wanting a man who's become as rude, arrogant and totally selfish as he has.

MRS. C. He seems much the same to me.

RUPERT. Thank you.

SARAH. You should have seen him earlier. He behaved atrociously and the sooner he's out of here the better.

MRS. C. Where will you go Rupert?

RUPERT. (*Coming out of the play.*) I'm not going anywhere until I've broken this bugger's neck!

(*The CAST once again are at a loss.*)

PROMPTER. (*Off.*) "I'm not going anywhere, my solicitor has advised me to stay ..."

MADGE. (*Trying to help.*) That's right, yes. I've advised him to stay.

RUPERT. (*Pursuing his own thoughts.*) I wouldn't listen to your advice for a second.

MRS. C. Where is he? What's he talking about?

RUPERT. I'm talking about an incident which took place after the matinee this afternoon. (*Grabs Madge's hand.*) My wife had a torrid little knock-up with this rat here. (*Points at Charles.*)

MADGE. (*Shaken.*) You mean your wife—Sarah?

RUPERT. Forget Sarah. Forget the play. I mean my wife—my real wife—you. You've been having it off with Charley boy.

MRS. C. I don't think we wish to know that.

RUPERT. Tough.

CHARLES. (*Desperately.*) Stick to the play.

RUPERT. I don't give a stuff about the play.

MRS. C. (*Nods in the direction of the audience.*) They do.

RUPERT. It's not exactly a masterpiece, is it? A couple split up, engage their friends to handle the divorce, and finish up swapping partners. Not what you'd call earth shattering.

MRS. C. It's amusingly written and there are some very good twists.

RUPERT. Not until the father-in-law turns up in the second act and gets a few easy laughs. And that's only on a good night when he's sober.

MRS. C. (*Outraged.*) How could you say such a thing?

RUPERT. Oh darling come off it. He's got a real problem. (*Makes a tippling gesture with his hand.*) Know what I mean?

MRS. C. A gentleman wouldn't mention it.

RUPERT. That's even worse than some of your real lines.

MRS. C. You needn't be so disparaging. It's as good as most plays—the set is attractive and there are no four letter words.

RUPERT. Up to this point.

MRS. C. Nor after it, as far as I remember.

RUPERT. I may just change all that.

MRS. C. You'll offend people.

RUPERT. Who?

MRS. C. I mean—you know—(*Indicates the audience.*)

RUPERT. I doubt if they'll walk out in droves. In fact you can hear a pin drop. Now do any of you have anything you wish to add before I warm to my theme?

MADGE. Not while you're upstaging us all.

RUPERT. I have every right—it's my scene for God's sake.

MADGE. You do it anyway.

RUPERT. Utterly untrue.

MADGE. Darling, when Charles has his line about—"we were thoroughly enjoying the pork en croute and then the balloon went up" he has his neck screwed round 180 degrees straight up the back wall.

RUPERT. He doesn't have to look at me, he can say it out front.

MADGE. You mean like you do.

RUPERT. (*Straight out front.*) When did I ever deliver my lines out front?

MADGE. There you go again. He used to get a laugh on that line.

RUPERT. When?

SARAH. On tour.

RUPERT. Darling, that's no criterion, you can get laughs in *Othello* on tour.

CHARLES. I didn't.

RUPERT. Perhaps you weren't at your best—worn out from having it away with Desdemona.

MADGE. (*Starts to go.*) I think you're mad.

RUPERT. Where are you going?

MADGE. I don't know—to my dressing room—anywhere.

RUPERT. Stay where you are.

MRS. C. If nobody minds, I think—I think I'll just walk off.

RUPERT. Not like you to leave the stage without a good exit line. I should wait until you find one.

(MRS CULLEN sits down in a huff.)

CHARLES. I think we should all just walk off.

RUPERT. I warn you once you step out of sight of this audience I shall probably throttle you.

CHARLES. (*To the prompt corner.*) If you can't ring the curtain down, then phone for a doctor, the poor chap's having a brainstorm.

RUPERT. You were in my wife's dressing room.

CHARLES. All right—yes—I was in there. What the hell does that prove? I mean we were having a perfectly innocent conversation.

RUPERT. So why lock the door?

CHARLES. It—it wasn't locked.

RUPERT. Don't lie—I tried it. (*Stops.*) Just a minute, when were you in *Othello*?

CHARLES. About twenty years ago.

RUPERT. Not in London.

CHARLES. I didn't say it was in London.

RUPERT. Some piddling little Rep. I suppose.

CHARLES. It was an overseas tour for the Old Vic.

RUPERT. Isle of Man—Jersey?

CHARLES. South America.

RUPERT. They probably didn't speak English.

CHARLES. I don't imagine you've ever been in Shakespeare.

RUPERT. You're quite right, I haven't. I know my limitations. A frothy little comedy is about my mark. I'm not very convincing when it comes to "tearing a passion to tatters."

MADGE. You're not doing too badly now.

RUPERT. Oh thank you. D'you think I should take it up?

MADGE. I don't see why not.

MRS. C. I doubt if any Management will ever employ you again after tonight.

RUPERT. Very good, dear. I should exit on that.

MRS. C. (*In desperation.*) I wonder if there's a doctor in the house.

RUPERT. (*Laughs.*) That's even better. You got a laugh. If you'd only been near the door and nipped off quickly, it could've been a round of applause

MRS. C. Have you no respect for the Theatre?

RUPERT. Forget the Theatre, we're in a real life situation. I'm me. You're you. And this man here is making a mockery of my marriage.

MRS. C. Why couldn't you wait until the intermission?

RUPERT. I'm beginning to find you a really stupid woman.

MRS. C. And I find you impossible.

RUPERT. Impossible.

MRS. C. You're rude, arrogant and totally selfish.

RUPERT. We've had that bit, can't you find some words of your own?

MADGE. Why bother? They sum you up perfectly.

RUPERT. I should think I have every right to be rude, but not half as rude as your boyfriend. And I would say that making love to someone else's wife smacks of arrogance, verging on the selfish.

CHARLES. We didn't make love!

MADGE. Yes, we did!

CHARLES. Well—I mean—you know—

RUPERT. No, we don't know. There seems to be a slight difference of opinion.

MADGE. No, there isn't.

CHARLES. Yes, there is.

RUPERT. Is this a problem of morals, or semantics?

MADGE. We love each other, that's enough.

CHARLES. Darling, you don't have to blurt it out in front of all these people.

RUPERT. These people or those people out there?

CHARLES. What's the difference?

RUPERT. We're getting it all for free up here.

CHARLES. Cheap little remarks—you always have to chip in with some footling comment.

RUPERT. I thought it was mildly amusing. Something to take the heat out of the moment. You should be grateful—(Nods towards the audience.) I'm sure they are.

MADGE. You never stop acting do you?

RUPERT. I had a very rough six months last year. If it hadn't been for that Andrex voice-over we'd've had to take Jason away from Marlborough.

MADGE. I never wanted him to go there in the first place.

RUPERT. Most actors want their children to go to a public school. It gives them respectability.

SARAH. The children, or the actors?

RUPERT. Actors of course.

MADGE. Well certainly not actresses. I don't set any store by respectability.

RUPERT. Obviously not. In view of your little ding-dong with lover boy.

MADGE. You just trivialize everything don't you?

RUPERT. I wouldn't have said that stopping a play dead in its tracks was trivial. More like momentous.

MADGE. Then let me tell you what I feel about my lover. I'll make that momentous too.

CHARLES. Darling—please—

RUPERT. You might embarrass him. (*To Charles.*) Would you like to make a bee-line for it?

CHARLES. No, I feel I ought to be around just to keep the record straight.

MADGE. We're lovers, there's no point in denying it. We're having an affair.

CHARLES. Well—yes—but there are gradations to an affair.

RUPERT. Look this seems to be your scene. Would you like to take the centre of the stage?

CHARLES. I'm all right where I am, thanks.

RUPERT. Please yourself. But do speak up a bit.

MADGE. Don't you give him notes, he's a better actor than you any day.

MRS. C. Hear, hear.

RUPERT. (*Rounding on her.*) The sooner you push off, the better.

MADGE. You can't stand the truth can you?

RUPERT. Try me, and we'll see. Go on.

MADGE. He was voted Actor of the Year in the Evening Standard Awards in nineteen—

RUPERT. (*Cutting in.*) I'm not talking about his bloody career. I mean his private life.

CHARLES. There's nothing much private about it now.

RUPERT. No, not any more. Go on, darling.

MADGE. He came to my dressing room.

RUPERT. Of his own accord, or had you invited him?

MADGE. I knew he was coming.

RUPERT. Don't fudge, I asked for the truth.

MADGE. He asked if he could see me between shows, and I said "yes."

RUPERT. Knowing what might happen?

MADGE. I hadn't thought that far. All I knew was that I felt strongly attracted to him.

RUPERT. More strongly than you do to me?

MADGE. Yes. I happened to be changing. I was just wearing my wrap when he came in. He embraced me and we kissed.

RUPERT. Passionately?

MADGE. Gently to begin with and then, well yes, passionately. And then before we realized what we were doing, he'd undressed.

RUPERT. (*Looks out front.*) That's got them firmly in their seats. And you didn't stop him?

MADGE. No, I'd always done so on previous occasions.

RUPERT. Previous occa—Oh God, I could do with a drink. (*HE automatically goes for the stage whisky bottle.*)

SARAH. You won't get much comfort from cold tea.

RUPERT. (*Shouts to the prompt corner.*) Angela! Angela!

(ANGELA enters.)

RUPERT. Go to my room and bring me the bottle of whisky.

ANGELA. I'm trying to ring the front of house manager.

RUPERT. What for?

ANGELA. To tell him what's happened.

RUPERT. I shouldn't bother. He'll either be in the pub, or cleared off with the takings. Just go and get that bottle, there's a good girl.

ANGELA. I'm not supposed to leave the prompt corner.

RUPERT. Who says?

ANGELA. It's just the rules of the theatre. The prompt corner has to be manned at all times.

RUPERT. That's if the play's in progress.

ANGELA. I can't leave until the curtain comes down.

SARAH. I'll get it for you. (*SARAH exits.*)

ANGELA. I'd like to help you, but I've only just got my Equity Card.

RUPERT. You really must learn to speak up if you want to be an actress, and I take it you do?

ANGELA. Oh yes.

RUPERT. Is this your first appearance on a stage?

ANGELA. Not really, I've done a few auditions.

RUPERT. Yes, well, you have to speak louder when there's an audience. They soak up the sound. Try again and project your voice. (*Demonstrates.*) "I've done a few auditions."

ANGELA. "I've done a few auditions."

RUPERT. You don't have to take the roof off. There's a subtle difference between projection and shouting. Unless of course you're doing Shakespeare and then, as our classical actor here will tell you, the more you rant and rave, the better. Anyway you better get back to your corner.

ANGELA. Thank you. (*ANGELA exits.*)

CHARLES. It's little wonder you never acted in Shakespeare.

RUPERT. That's pretty rich, being criticised by a man who's just been enjoying himself stark-naked with my wife.

CHARLES. I was not enjoying myself!!

RUPERT. Then you're a bigger fool than I thought.

CHARLES. What I mean is nothing happened.

RUPERT. Oh. Didn't you like what you saw?

CHARLES. Don't be an idiot. Of course I did. She's divine. She's the most wonderful woman in the world and I love her a damned sight more than you do.

RUPERT. So what brought you up—as they say—short?

CHARLES. We heard somebody at the door.

RUPERT. Oh dear—my fault. I apologise.

MADGE. You don't mean it—so why say it?

RUPERT. What are you supposed to say in this sort of situation? I mean I'd happily kill him, but it might upset one or two people.

MRS. C. It would be very out of character as well.

RUPERT. You think so?

MRS. C. You'd only do that if the balance of your mind is disturbed.

CHARLES. I'm not so sure it isn't.

RUPERT. And I have grave doubts about yours. Any man who can strip for action in between the shows, with the whole of the cast and the backstage staff floating about, shows a recklessness verging on insanity.

MADGE. You hypocrite!

RUPERT. I beg your pardon?

MADGE. You seem to forget the first time you made love to me.

RUPERT. I may have. Refresh my memory.

MADGE. In my dressing-room of the Playhouse, Weston super Mare.

RUPERT. Weston super Mare?

MADGE. When we were touring in *Private Lives.*

RUPERT. Oh yes, well as far as I remember it wasn't very successful.

MADGE. I became pregnant.

RUPERT. I meant the tour.

MRS. C. I played that in the West End once, and Noel Coward came round to see me afterwards. He said I was enchanting.

RUPERT. I'll bet he kept his clothes on.

MADGE. You revel in a cheap laugh. You always did.

RUPERT. That's what the customers pay for. May as well give them one occasionally.

(SARAH enters with a bottle of whisky.)

RUPERT. Ah, ministering angel. (*HE takes the bottle and pours a neat whisky.*)

SARAH. I'm sorry I've been so long, but I've been trying to put Edward in the picture.

RUPERT. Oh poor old Edward—yes. Is he in his normal happy state? (*MIMES a tippling hand.*)

SARAH. I'm afraid so. But he says he's got his new agent out front tonight, so he hopes it'll go particularly well.

RUPERT. (*Knocks the whisky back.*) It never rains—

CHARLES. (*Angrily to Rupert.*) You would have to choose today wouldn't you?

RUPERT. I might say the same to you.

MADGE. He's a dear sweet lovely man.

RUPERT. And a soak. (*HE pours himself another drink.*)

MADGE. He was a bigger star than you could ever be.

RUPERT. I swear before the night's out I may kill both of you. (*HE knocks back another whisky.*)

CHARLES. (*Shouts to the prompt corner.*) Angela, for God's sake get the curtain down.

ANGELA. (*Off.*) What?

CHARLES. Push the bloody button.

ANGELA. (*Off.*) I'm trying to find the phone number of the pub!!

RUPERT. Go and ask Edward, he practically lives there.

MRS. C. It might surprise you to know that his was one of the finest "Lears" I ever saw.

RUPERT. Was it in your direction dear?

MRS. C. Your wife was right, you'll stoop to any depth for a titter.

MADGE. The poor old boy's had a rotten patch lately.

MRS. C. Only because he has trouble learning his lines. On his day he's still magic.

RUPERT. I haven't seen much sign of it in this.

CHARLES. What do you expect? He's only got a spit and a cough in the second act.

RUPERT. No such thing as a small part—only small actors.

MADGE. You should know.

RUPERT. That was pretty cheap—in fact, in your case, downright dangerous.

CHARLES. I don't think she really meant it.

RUPERT. Oh don't you? I suppose you think you understand my wife better than I do.

CHARLES. Possibly, but this is what is laughingly called a team play. No damned good for the actor. No kudos whatsoever no starring roles, we just get lost in the crowd.

RUPERT. Except for our divine "Sarah." She won an award for the best supporting comedy actress.

SARAH. Awards are invidious things.

RUPERT. (*Pours another whisky.*) Don't tell us you regret having it?

SARAH. No, of course not.

MRS. C. Get 'em while you can dear.

SARAH. (*To Mrs. C.*) It should have gone to you.

MRS. C. (*Rather agreeing.*) Ah, well—

RUPERT. Nonsense. You've got a certain quality, people find you mesmeric.

MADGE. Including you.

RUPERT. Yes, including me.

MADGE. Do you fancy her?

RUPERT. Don't change the subject. (*HE drinks.*)

MADGE. You do.

RUPERT. Along with most men—but we're not going to rush round to her dressing-room after the show and strip down to our socks. (*Bears down on Charles.*) Like some people.

CHARLES. Keep away. You're mad.

MADGE. And drunk.

RUPERT. On two whiskies!!

MADGE. Three.

MRS. C. And probably some before the curtain went up.

RUPERT. I'm rapidly going off you.

CHARLES. No wonder he forgot his lines.

SARAH. He didn't touch a drop.

MADGE. How would you know?

SARAH. Because I was with him.

MRS. C. Ah! The plot thickens.

RUPERT. The plot, my dear old bat, went out of the window twenty minutes ago.

MRS. C. (*Rises.*) I don't have to take insults like that from you.

RUPERT. No you don't. You can make a dramatic exit. And if you come up with a good line I'll start a round of applause for you.

MRS. C. You—you treat me like a door-mat.

RUPERT. You've already tried that one, and it wasn't any more successful then.

MRS. C. If I walk off you'll only say something rude to my back.

RUPERT. It can take it—it's broad enough.

(*MRS CULLEN sits again.*)

MADGE. I would like to know what our award-winning actress was doing in your dressing-room.

RUPERT. Said she—switching from defense to attack.

MADGE. Well go on, I'm sure we'd all like to hear.

MRS. C. Yes, we would.

RUPERT. (*To Mrs. Cullen.*) I'm sure in a previous life you used to knit.

MRS C. Knit?

RUPERT. At the foot of the guillotine.

MADGE. You haven't answered my question.

RUPERT. It's completely irrelevant.

MADGE. You've already admitted you fancy her.

RUPERT. I fancy Diane Sawyer but it's not indictable. And its certainly no excuse for you to leap onto the couch with lover-boy.

(*A St. John's AMBULANCE NURSE walks onto the stage. SHE blinks in the lights and looks totally out of place.*)

RUPERT. What the hell do you want?

NURSE. I was on duty in the front of house when somebody asked for a doctor.

RUPERT. Yes I believe it was one of "Mrs. C's" more memorable lines.

NURSE. As no one seems to have come forward I thought I better offer my services.

MRS. C. I don't think they'll be required somehow.

RUPERT. How the hell do you know? There could be a man lying here gasping for life and mercy at any moment.

(*To the nurse.*) Are you adept at mouth to mouth resuscitation?

NURSE. It does figure in our training manual, yes. But there's been no call for it so far. Not in the Dress Circle anyway.

MRS. C. I doubt if there'll be any need for it here either. So I should return to your post.

RUPERT. You just don't want another character woman on the stage stealing the limelight.

CHARLES. (*Shouts.*) Angela for God's sake, get this damn curtain down.

ANGELA. (*Off.*) I can't find the phone number of The Salisbury.

CHARLES. They don't go to The Salisbury they go to the Marquis of Granby!

ANGELA. (*Off.*) How do you spell it?

RUPERT. No wonder she went into the theatre.

CHARLES. I'll find it for you.

(*HE starts to go. RUPERT pulls out a gun from his pocket.*)

RUPERT. You take one step off this stage and I'll shoot.

CHARLES. (*Hesitates.*) That's a prop which we use in the second act.

NURSE. Yes, it gets quite a laugh sometimes.

RUPERT. (*Stung.*) Sometimes?! Always!

NURSE. No, not always. I've seen this play—oh—about a hundred times I suppose, and some nights you don't get so much as a titter.

MRS. C. (*Beaming.*) She can stay.

RUPERT. Everyone's a bloody critic ...

NURSE. Oh I wouldn't go so far as to put myself in that bracket. But I have noticed that if you happen to produce the gun before you say your line about "a shot in the dark"—it's not half as funny as when you say the line first.

MRS. C. She's quite right.

RUPERT. (*To the nurse.*) Would you kindly leave the stage?

MADGE. I think she ought to remain where she is.

CHARLES. (*To Madge.*) Don't worry darling, I can handle a deranged man with a toy gun.

RUPERT. (*Goes to the desk.*) How do you feel about a toy paper-knife? (*HE picks up the knife.*)

MADGE. Put that down.

MRS. C. It's just another prop.

RUPERT. Yes, just another prop. (*HE throws it and it digs into the desk and is obviously lethal.*)

CHARLES. Angela!

ANGELA. (*Off.*) What?

CHARLES. It's M-A-R-Q-U-I-S. (*Spelling it out.*)

ANGELA. (*Off.*) What is?

CHARLES. The Marquis of sodding Granby!

MRS. C. (*Rises.*) Do you mind? There are ladies present.

RUPERT. If you don't like the heat in the kitchen, piss off.

MRS. C. (*Sits abruptly.*) I was thinking about our audience, not to mention the nurse here.

NURSE. It's all right. I did a season at the Royal Court.

RUPERT. I think they'll all survive. They'll see another day. But I'm not so sure about lover-boy. (*HE picks up the knife again.*)

MADGE. Don't be so stupid. I keep telling you that nothing happened.

RUPERT. You don't keep telling me at all, you told me once.

MADGE. Well I'm telling you again.

RUPERT. Why should I believe you?

NURSE. Because she's your wife.

RUPERT. You seem to have missed the gist of our problems. Have you been sitting out there all this time?

NURSE. Apart from when I had a cup of coffee in the Circle Bar. I always pop in there for a few minutes in the first act.

RUPERT. Well it may surprise you to know, Mrs.—er—er

NURSE. Brown.

RUPERT. Mrs Brown.

NURSE. *Miss* Brown actually.

RUPERT. Oh, well it may surprise you even more, *Miss* Brown to know that my wife and our friend here were cavorting about between the matinee and the evening performance stark naked.

NURSE. (*Shocked.*) I can barely believe such a thing.

RUPERT. (*With a laugh to Mrs. C.*) I'll bet you wish *you'd* said that.

MRS. C. I've always suspected that you don't like me very much.

RUPERT. I'll admit there's one person here I don't like very much but it's not you.

MADGE. I've told you—nothing took place.

RUPERT. What do you mean by nothing?

MADGE. We didn't make love.

CHARLES. We were together, I admit it, but nothing more.

RUPERT. No. Perhaps you just embraced, touched each other.

CHARLES and MADGE. (*Together.*) No/Yes.

RUPERT. Try again.

MADGE. How can we remember? It was very confused.

RUPERT. Only after you heard someone try the door. Before that it must've been ecstatic. (*No response.*) Well wasn't it? You saw each other. You touched each other. You embraced. Flesh upon flesh. That's what love is, seeing and touching. And then the highlights. Some perfect—some perfectly absurd. Probably in your lover's case it would've been the latter.

MADGE. It's only jealousy that makes you say that.

RUPERT. Rubbish. I'll bet that little interruption of mine was just the excuse he needed to pull back, he didn't have to prove his manhood. Total collapse of stout party.

MADGE. That's not true. (*To Charles.*) Tell him it's not true.

CHARLES. (*Hesitates.*) Well—

RUPERT. Don't drive the poor sod into a corner. The whole episode was a non-event. He can't cut the mustard. Right? Admit it.

CHARLES. Yes, all right. We've told you. Nothing happened.

RUPERT. Nor ever could.

MADGE. Utterly untrue!

CHARLES. Darling—please—

MADGE. He's a magnificent lover! We have made love wildly, gloriously and frequently!!

CHARLES. (*Resigned.*) Oh God.

MADGE. He could give you lessons

RUPERT. It may be a touch late, because right now I could plunge this knife into him so easily it almost frightens me.

MRS. C. Unbalanced—I thought so.

RUPERT. D'you know, for once you could be right. How's your first aid when it comes to dealing with knife wounds Miss Brown?

NURSE. Well—I—I would have to try and recall some of my earlier lectures.

RUPERT. Don't worry, if you lose this patient it won't be the end of the world.

MRS. C. Except for him.

RUPERT. You keep trotting them out don't you?

MADGE. I suggest we all walk off.

CHARLES. No, let's stick it out here.

RUPERT. Good thinking old man. He knows he's relatively safe in full view of the customers. The last person to be killed in front of an audience was Abraham Lincoln. (*RUPERT walks towards Charles.*) Or shall we up-date history?

MADGE. Please put that knife down.

RUPERT. No.

MADGE. Very well. (*SHE opens the steamer trunk and turns to Charles.*) Get in there.

CHARLES. What?

MADGE. Just get in.

CHARLES. Why?

MADGE. Because you'll be out of harm's way—that's why.

CHARLES. Damnit, I'm not in a French farce.

RUPERT. Nor ever likely to be either.

CHARLES. (*Stung.*) I'm magnificent in farce!

RUPERT. Then prove it. (*HE threatens Charles with the knife.*)

MADGE. Please, get in, I beg you.

CHARLES. Oh very well.

(*CHARLES gets into the trunk and MADGE closes it.*)

MRS. C. The poor man'll suffocate.

RUPERT. And by his lover's hand. We've gone from French farce to Greek tragedy. They're certainly getting their money's worth.

ANGELA. (*Rushes on and looks up to the flies.*) Curtain!

VOICE. (*From the flies.*) I haven't had the cue yet!

ANGELA. There won't be one! Just drop it in.

(*THE CURTAIN begins to descend slowly.*)

RUPERT. (*To the flies.*) Get it up you fool! Up! They'll miss the best part!!

CURTAIN

ACT II

*The same. VOICES are heard on stage as the CURTAIN
RISES. The CAST are still on stage. SARAH is seated
U.R. facing upstage.*

MRS. C. It's high time he came out of there.

RUPERT. I'm not stopping him.

MADGE. Of course you are. (*Suddenly realizes the
curtain is up.*) Angela, what the hell have you raised the
curtain for?

ANGELA. (*Enters.*) What?

MADGE. Why raise the curtain?

ANGELA. I thought the audience would've gone by
now.

MADGE. Well they haven't, have they?

RUPERT. Can you blame them? There's a little matter
of a body in a trunk. It's always a crowd puller.

MRS. C. Only when it's a dead one.

RUPERT. The night is young.

ANGELA. He could suffocate?

MADGE. He's all right. (*Raises her voice to the trunk.*)
You're still all right, aren't you?

CHARLES. What?

MADGE. (*Opens the trunk a little.*) I said are you still
breathing?

CHARLES. Yes, but I'm getting cramp.

MRS. C. Rub your calves.

CHARLES. There's very little elbow room.

43

NURSE. (*Enters cheerfully.*) I've been listening to the audience in the Bars and they seem to be enjoying it far more than usual.

MRS. C. (*Rather pleased.*) Really?

RUPERT. Hardly surprising, the plot's greatly improved and we've all got better parts.

CHARLES. I'm buggered if I have.

RUPERT. You wait, your death scene could be a "tour de force."

ANGELA. Shall I get them to drop the curtain again?

MADGE. No, leave it up. My husband wouldn't be mad enough to try anything in full view of the audience.

RUPERT. Don't bank on it. A "Crime Passionelle" always arouses a certain amount of sympathy with the average jury and I'd say the one we have tonight is fairly representative. I'm sure they feel it would be justifiable homicide.

MRS. C. Angela dear, where on earth is the Manager?

ANGELA. I still can't get hold of him.

RUPERT. He's probably having it off with an usherette.

MADGE. Now you can see the crudeness of the man.

RUPERT. Ye gods! You accuse me of being crude, when you admit to humping about with "steamer-trunk Charlie"!!

MRS. C. May I remind you that there are ladies present?!

RUPERT. Not one of your better lines, but if you promise to make your exit, I'll start your applause. (*HE begins to clap.*) Off you go.

MRS. C. I'm not leaving until you decide to behave in a civilised manner, and simply ask for a divorce.

RUPERT. Why the hell would I do that?

MRS. C. Because you obviously don't love each other.

RUPERT. You couldn't be more wrong. It's precisely because I *do* love her that I'm prepared to wipe out the opposition.

MADGE. You don't love me at all, you just enjoy the role of the aggrieved husband, and going way over the top as usual with your over-acting.

RUPERT. (*Outrages.*) I never over-act!

MADGE. What d'you think you're doing now?

RUPERT. (*Picks up the whisky bottle and pours another drink.*) My problem is I don't know which one of you to kill first.

NURSE. I hardly think another drink would be advisable.

RUPERT. Piss off.

MRS. C. I've told you already we don't like four-letter words.

RUPERT. All right, bugger off, and you can join her.

MADGE. You don't love anyone except yourself.

RUPERT. I love you.

NURSE But you've just threatened to kill her—it's not very logical.

RUPERT. Oh do shut up.

SARAH. All men destroy the thing they love.

RUPERT. (*Noticing Sarah.*) I'd forgotten you were still there.

MADGE. Don't try and make excuses for him, he's a mess.

SARAH. I think he's magnificent.

RUPERT. Ah. She didn't win her award as best supporting actress for nothing.

CHARLES. Ask her why she was in his dressing room before the show.

RUPERT. That's a bit of a liberty, coming from you.

MADGE. (*To Sarah.*) Are you in love with my husband?

SARAH. Yes—but he doesn't know it.

MRS. C. Well, he knows now.

RUPERT. I wish you'd stop putting your oar in.

MADGE. She loves you darling.

RUPERT. (*Thrown.*) Yes—well—it's very sweet of her—I'm enormously flattered—I really am—but it's not the issue at stake, is it?

MADGE. I think it is. She's young, attractive, beautiful figure, eager lips. But I expect you've tasted them already.

RUPERT. A polite peck on the cheek, that's all.

MADGE. In your dressing room?

RUPERT. I can't say exactly say where, saying good-night at the stage door or in the pub, possibly in the street: I can't remember. But it's just casual—polite—nothing deeply significant. I mean we all do it, don't we? I even kiss Old Mother Riley here.

MRS. C. I don't enjoy it.

RUPERT. Snap!!

SARAH. Kiss me now.

RUPERT. What?

SARAH. (*Embraces him.*) Please—please—kiss me.

RUPERT. There are people watching.

SARAH. You were prepared to kill in front of them, why not a kiss?

RUPERT. Well, that's different.

SARAH. I want you—I understand you—kiss me.

(SHE pulls him onto her lips. HE then gives in and kisses her passionately.)

CHARLES. Did he kiss her?
MADGE. Yes. And he's still kissing her.
CHARLES. Bloody cheek.

(CHARLES emerges from the trunk, as SARAH and RUPERT break from their kiss.)

SARAH. I'm sorry.
RUPERT. Please don't be.
SARAH. I just had to do it.
RUPERT. Yes—well—thank you.
MADGE. That's not much of a speech, you can do better than that surely? I'm sure we'd all like to hear your feelings on this rather unlikely turn of events.
CHARLES. And is it the first time it's happened, we ask ourselves?
RUPERT. Then you can damn well answer yourselves.
MRS. C. I would think the assumption is "no" considering he's already admitted he's strongly attracted to her.
MADGE. I can't remember the last time you kissed me like that.
RUPERT. Nor I.
CHARLES. If there's been a cooling off, then I suggest we look no further than our "divine Sarah."
RUPERT. *(Cutting in.)* Cooling off? Who said there'd been a cooling off?
MRS. C. He said "if" there had.

RUPERT. He's no right to be saying anything at all. Get back in the bloody trunk.

CHARLES. Oh for Christ's sake.

RUPERT. No, for yours. (*Picks up the paper knife.*) Go on.

MADGE. Darling, why can't you face the fact that I don't love you and she does?

RUPERT. Because "darling" one sensuous kiss does not wipe out fifteen years of marriage, or if it does then the entire audience will be heading for the Divorce Court.

MRS. C. Your wife, it appears, has gone way beyond a passionate kiss.

RUPERT. I may still forgive her.

CHARLES. (*Somewhat relieved.*) Ah, at last a sign of magnanimity.

RUPERT. I didn't say anything about forgiving *you.*

(*RUPERT bears down on CHARLES who quickly gets back into the trunk, which remains slightly open.*)

NURSE. Will you please put that knife down?

RUPERT. No I won't.

NURSE. What if there's an accident?

RUPERT. There won't be. It'll be quite deliberate.

MADGE. You're insane.

RUPERT. I feel perfectly normal.

MRS. C. I can't see anything normal about forgiving your wife, if you're all set to murder her lover.

CHARLES. Don't encourage him.

MRS. C. Well I think someone should point out the illogicality. He'd be dead, you'd be in prison and your wife would go off with someone else.

CHARLES. Will you stop harping on death!

ANGELA. (*Walks on.*) Mr. Frobisher's in the wings waiting to make his entrance.

MADGE. Doesn't he realise what's happened?

ANGELA. I've tried to tell him but it's not easy with him being so deaf.

RUPERT. Or drunk?

ANGELA. Oh I don't think he's any worse than usual.

RUPERT. That's not saying much.

ANGELA. He thinks he's missed his entrance cue.

RUPERT. He generally does.

MRS. C. That's grossly unfair, he's only done it twice.

RUPERT. There are dozens of actors, good actors, who wouldn't have done it at all. Why do we have to be lumbered with him?

MRS. C. Because he still has a name you can put above the title, and that's what puts bums on the seats dear.

RUPERT. (*In mock disgust.*) Another of those dreadful four-letter words.

MRS. C. I shall make it a point never to act with you again.

RUPERT. Promise?

ANGELA. He says he hopes it's going well because his agent's out front tonight.

MADGE. Then we should spare him the indignity of coming on. Who gives him his cue?

CHARLES. I do, when I say "Y-E-S." (*Spelling it out.*)

MADGE. Well don't say it.

CHARLES. No.

MRS. C. If I were his agent I should've left by now.

RUPERT. Rubbish. He's probably enjoying every minute of it. Bloody sight better than those boring revivals of Brecht and Shakespeare in track suits and gym shoes.

MRS. C. You obviously never saw me in the *Caucasian Chalk Circle* or *Mother Earth.*

RUPERT. No. In fact I studiously avoided them.

MRS. C. Nothing to be proud of.

RUPERT. Then I'm surprised you mentioned them.

MRS. C. Your cheap cynicism is beginning to get on my tits.

RUPERT. Language, Mother dear.

MADGE. (*To Angela.*) Just try and keep Edward off.

ANGELA. I can't be everywhere at once. (*ANGELA exits.*)

NURSE. (*Trying to pour oil on troubled waters.*) I'm sure we'd all feel a lot safer if you put that knife down.

RUPERT. I dare say you would especially our friend in the trunk, which is precisely why I shall hang on to it.

CHARLES. It's damned hot in here.

RUPERT. Then sweat.

NURSE. With all this lighting he could get heatstroke.

RUPERT. No problem, I can stab a few extra holes in the side. (*HE moves to do so.*)

CHARLES. No—don't!!

RUPERT. Oh, you've got enough air, have you?

CHARLES. Yes.

RUPERT. Sure?

CHARLES. (*Loudly.*) Yes!!

(*EDWARD hearing his cue enters. HE has had more to drink than usual but hides it well. And being blissfully unaware that anything is amiss he carries on with the*

original play. The CAST rally round loyally for the
sake of Edward and his agent and revert to the play.)

EDWARD. Did you know your front door was open?

SARAH. No Dad, we didn't.

EDWARD. You ought to be more careful.

MRS. C. Why aren't you at home?

EDWARD. The weather was so bloody awful I thought
I'd prefer to be in the peaceful bosom of my family.

SARAH. It's not particularly peaceful right now.

EDWARD. Since you mention it, there does seem to be
a slight tension in the air.

MRS. C. Rupert wants to leave Sarah.

EDWARD. Well before he does, perhaps he'd be kind
enough to offer me a drink.

RUPERT. Help yourself.

EDWARD. Thank you. (*HE pours himself a drink from
the real whisky bottle.*)

SARAH. And before you chip in with fatherly advice I
think I ought to tell you that Mother is all in favour of us
parting.

EDWARD. It may interest you to know that your
Mother and I decided to do exactly the same thing twenty
years ago. And look at us now.

MRS. C. Regretting every moment of it.

EDWARD. (*Knocks back his whisky which takes him
by surprise.*) Christ.

MRS. C. And Charles and Madge are handling all the
divorce proceedings.

EDWARD. Oh well that keeps it nicely in the family.
(*HE helps himself to another whisky.*) How are you
Madge?

MADGE. Fine thanks.

EDWARD. You look younger every time I see you. (*HE knocks back his whisky.*)

MADGE. Thank you.

MRS. C. He says that to our "daily."

EDWARD. And how's the world treating you Charles? (*Looks round for Charles.*) Charles?

CHARLES. (*Raising his voice.*) Mustn't complain, business is pretty brisk!

EDWARD. (*Stares hard at the trunk. Totally lost.*) What er—(*HE turns and comes face to face with the nurse.*) Good God, I mean good evening.

NURSE. Good evening, sir.

MRS. C. (*Trying to rescue him.*) This is Nurse Brown.

EDWARD. (*Lost.*) Who?

MRS. C. Nurse Brown. She's just popped in.

EDWARD. Oh.

(*THERE is a pause. MADGE tries to feed him his line.*)

MADGE. You don't seem particularly surprised.

EDWARD. I'm *very* surprised. I don't remember her at all.

MADGE. No. About the situation.

EDWARD. What?

MRS C. Between Rupert and your daughter.

EDWARD. (*Back on track.*) Ah yes. I'm not particularly surprised that this marriage has hit the rocks. In fact it's remarkable it didn't happen sooner, given that Sarah's a highly intelligent sensitive girl and Rupert's a conceited twit.

RUPERT. I rather regret offering you that drink.

EDWARD. Well as you're not liable to do it again I better help myself. (*HE pours another whisky.*)

MRS. C. (*To herself.*) Fatal.

MADGE. If you felt that way about Rupert why agree to the marriage?

EDWARD. I suppose he was no worse than all the other conceited twits who came roaring up on motor-bikes to claim her hand.

RUPERT. In my case it was a two-seater M.G.

EDWARD. Ah yes, the cad's motor car. I got your number then young man.

SARAH. It's a pity you didn't say so at the time.

EDWARD. No point. You and your Mother had caught wedding fever and there was nothing I could've said to stop you.

MRS. C. You have a conveniently short memory my darling. I launched us all into that marriage to save our own.

EDWARD. Careful dear, strangers present.

MRS C. I had to do something to prevent you waltzing off with the bar-maid at the golf club.

EDWARD. Oh darling, give me credit.

MRS. C. She gave you plenty.

RUPERT. Fascinating.

EDWARD. A mild flirtation.

MRS. C. A full blooded affair.

RUPERT. And he didn't even own an M.G.

SARAH. My God, I wish I'd known. My whole marriage has been based on a lie.

EDWARD. Nothing unusual about that. A lot of 'em are and work very well.

SARAH. I hope you'll make full use of these facts in my divorce Charles.

CHARLES. It's certainly all grist to the mill.

EDWARD. (*Stares at the trunk.*) He's in a trunk.

MADGE. (*Pressing on.*) I have to remind you that a hastily contrived marriage works equally well in favour of *my* client.

RUPERT. Touché.

EDWARD. What's he doing in a trunk?

MRS. C. (*Ploughing on.*) I could've sued for divorce I suppose, but in my day we tried hard to lock our skeletons in a cupboard.

EDWARD. We've got one here in a fucking trunk!!

NURSE. Language, please.

EDWARD. Are we in Act Two?

RUPERT. Yes old man, but it's a different plot.

EDWARD. Oh God, the actor's nightmare. (*HE sinks into a chair.*)

MRS. C. Did you have to confuse the poor man in front of everyone?

RUPERT. He had to know sooner or later.

MRS. C. You only had to wait for his big speech on the next page and then he exits, and very often to a round of applause.

RUPERT. I've never understood why.

NURSE. Because on the nights when I'm on duty here, I start it.

RUPERT. How much does he pay you?

MRS. C. Only you could make such a despicable remark.

RUPERT. I don't blame him. I'm just curious—that's all.

NURSE. I've been a devout fan of Mr. Frobisher for more years than I care to remember.

EDWARD. A compliment I could do without.

NURSE. I was privileged to see his "Shylock" at the Old Vic.

RUPERT. Shylock? How did it compare with Henry Irving?

EDWARD. (*Angrily to Rupert.*) Bastard.

RUPERT. I thought that was King John.

MADGE. How would you know? You've never been in Shakespeare.

RUPERT. True: but many a time and oft I've walked out of it.

EDWARD. What the hell's eating you?

RUPERT. A canker, Edward, that canker in yonder trunk.

EDWARD. What?

RUPERT. Not only "paddling palms and pinching fingers" but humping the daylights out of my beloved wife.

EDWARD. Oh frailty thy name is woman.

RUPERT. I'll lay six to four he's played Hamlet as well.

EDWARD. No lad, only Horatio.

MRS. C. And very good you were too.

NURSE. Memorable.

EDWARD. Nobody's memorable in Horatio. I was a fool to accept it. You don't stand a hope in hell with that part. It's not called Hamlet for nothing. Claudius isn't bad—he has his moments, and that old prick Polonius steals what's left. If you don't play Hamlet you may as well stay in the pub and walk on at the end as fucking Fortinbras. (*HE knocks back the remains of his whisky.*)

MRS. C. Your "Lear" is still remembered.

EDWARD. It might've been but I had the misfortune to play it in an era that saw Wolfit, Gielgud and Olivier. Who remembers Frobisher?

CHARLES. I do.

EDWARD. Why doesn't he come out of that bloody trunk?

MADGE. Because my husband may kill him if he does.

EDWARD. Well I refuse to keep screwing my head upstage and talking to a dis-embodied voice. He's stealing the scene.

MADGE. There is no scene.

EDWARD. What?

MRS. C. The play's finished.

EDWARD. Then bring the curtain down. (*Shouts.*) Angela! Curtain.

ANGELA. (*Appears in the corner.*) It's no good. I've pressed the button but they've gone back to the pub.

EDWARD. I think I'll join them.

RUPERT. No need, there's still a drop left in the bottle. (*HE offers it to Edward.*)

EDWARD. Ah—thanks.

MADGE. Don't give him any more.

EDWARD. On second thoughts, better not, got someone in tonight. (*Taps his nose.*) No names, no packdrill.

SARAH. I think you should go now.

EDWARD. (*Pouring another drink.*) I'm not ready to go yet.

SARAH. Please.

EDWARD. What are you talking about? Those aren't
the lines—I thought you were my daughter.

SARAH. Not any more.

EDWARD. (*Reverts to King Lear. And does so with
gusto*).

Let it be so: thy truth then by thy dower.
For by the sacred radiance of the sun
The mysteries of Hecate and the night
By all the operation of the orbs
From who do exist and cease to be;
Here I disclaim all my paternal care,
Propinquity and property of blood,
And as a stranger to my heart and me
Hold me from this forever. The barbarous Scythian
Or he that makes this generation messes
To gorge his appetite, shall to my bosom
Be as well neighbour'd, pitied and relieved
As thou my sometime daughter

(*HE takes a drink.*)

CHARLES. (*Emerging from the trunk.*) Good my
Liege—

EDWARD. Peace Kent!

Come not between the dragon and his wrath.
I loved her most, and thought to set my rest
On her kind nursery. Hence and avoid my sight!
So be my grave my peace, as here I give
Her father's heart from her! Call France. Who stirs:?
Call Burgundy!

RUPERT. Call the Manager! Get him off!!

EDWARD. What?

RUPERT. Very good. We'll let you know.

MRS. C. Philistine!!

RUPERT. Oh don't you start.

EDWARD. (*Totally confused.*) What happened, where am I?

MRS. C. You were Lear—Edward.

RUPERT. Or possibly Edward Lear.

MADGE. (*Angrily.*) That's right, that's typical—mock everything you can't do, or appreciate.

RUPERT. I don't need a lecture from you on my shortcomings.

MADGE. Oh so you do admit you've got some.

RUPERT. Yes. And one of them was loving you.

MADGE. The only person you could ever really love is yourself.

RUPERT. You'd like to believe that because it salves your conscience.

MADGE. That's not true.

RUPERT. Balls. It justified your furtive little frolics with lover-boy.

MADGE. We have a passion for each other which you and I never had and never could have.

RUPERT. Oh. Strong stuff. (*Turns to Charles.*) And how say you—"Good my Liege"?

CHARLES. (*Gaining confidence.*) I shall love her for the rest of my life.

RUPERT. (*Picks up the knife again.*) Then I'd say you're going to have to pack a lot of passion into the next five minutes.

EDWARD. Is this a dagger I see before me?

RUPERT. No old boy, just a paper knife, but a blade by any other name would kill as sweet. You see, we can all do it.

SARAH. Put it down.

RUPERT. No.

SARAH. Please.

RUPERT. Why should I?

SARAH. I understand how you feel but let them go. I'll give you everything she's given you and more.

EDWARD. I say—steady on.

SARAH. (*Embraces Rupert.*) Hold me—feel me.

RUPERT. (*In two minds.*) Just a minute—

SARAH. Feel my warmth—my body—my love.

EDWARD. I don't remember this bit.

SARAH. Don't interrupt!

EDWARD. (*Back into "Lear."*)
I prithee daughter
Do not make me mad!

RUPERT. He's off again!

EDWARD.
I will not trouble thee my child, farewell
We'll no more meet, no more see one another
But yet thou art my flesh, my blood, my daughter
Or rather a disease that's in my flesh
Which I must needs call mine. Thou art a boil
A plague—sore, an embossed carbuncle,
In my corrupted blood. But I'll not chide thee
Let shame come when it will, I do not call it.
I do not bid the thunder-bearer shoot,
Nor tell tales of thee to high-judging Jove
Mend when thou canst. Be better at they leisure
I can be patient.

RUPERT. Well I can't. So sit down and shut up, or go off.

EDWARD. (*With his hand to his head.*) I don't feel very well.

MRS. C. It's all right Edward, the nurse is here.

NURSE. Come with me, Mr. Frobisher.

EDWARD. Ah, the times are out of joint.

NURSE. That's right dear. We'll have a little lie down shall we? (*SHE helps him towards the door.*)

EDWARD. May flights of angels sing thee to thy rest.

NURSE. That would be nice.

(EDWARD and the NURSE exit.)

MRS. C. (*To Rupert.*) You didn't have to humiliate him like that.

RUPERT. You're quite right, I didn't, he can do it all by himself. He's a walking disaster, stewed to the eyeballs.

MADGE. And who gave him real whisky?

RUPERT. Don't be so bloody stupid. He came on pissed.

MRS. C. He might possibly have had a little sip tonight—

RUPERT. Tonight—and every night.

MADGE. At least he's never forgotten his lines and brought the play to a dead stop and then poured out his petty little problems.

RUPERT. So you think infidelity's petty?

MADGE. It is where you are concerned.

RUPERT. Oh thank you.

MADGE. You mock everything—you always have. You've got no depth, nor warmth. It's not surprising I looked for it elsewhere. I've felt very lonely being married to you.

RUPERT. Why haven't you said so before?

MADGE. What would be the point? One doesn't criticise "God."

RUPERT. (*Turns to the cast.*) Did you get that? That wonderfully twisted female logic. She's guilty, but I'm the one who gets pilloried.

MADGE. More trivia. When you're cornered and have to face the facts you snipe and sneer at women.

RUPERT. Utterly untrue and you know it. I adore women.

MRS. C. I haven't seen much sign of it!

RUPERT. I make an exception in your case.

MADGE. Oh you may fancy one occasionally, but that hardly comes under the category of love.

RUPERT. And you know all about love, do you?

MADGE. (*SHE takes Charles's hand.*) I do now.

RUPERT. Ah—so he's taught you a few tricks has he?

MADGE. I may be unfaithful but you're just crude.

RUPERT. No darling, merely honest. "To me the whole business is vastly over-rated and always has been. I enjoy it for what it's worth and what is more, I fully intend to go on enjoying it for as long as anyone is interested. And when the time comes that they're not, I shall be perfectly content to settle down with an apple and a good book."

MRS. C. (*Accusingly.*) That's straight out of *Present Laughter*.

RUPERT. Don't be such an old fussy-knickers. At least it gets a chuckle which is more than can be said for bloody Lear.

CHARLES. Nothing's sacred to you, is it?

RUPERT. Hark who's talking—

CHARLES. No matter what you say, I love her.

RUPERT. You're going to stick to that, are you?

CHARLES. Yes.

RUPERT. At the risk of losing your life?

CHARLES. Yes!

EDWARD. (*Receiving his cue again, enters as though for the first time.*) Did you know your front door was open?

SARAH. Er—no Dad we didn't.

EDWARD. You ought to be more careful.

RUPERT. Get off!!

EDWARD. What?

MRS. C. (*Brightly.*) Why aren't you at home playing golf?

EDWARD. The weather was so bloody awful I thought I'd prefer to be in the peaceful bosom of my family.

SARAH. It's not particularly peaceful right now.

EDWARD. Since you mention it, there does seem to be a slight tension in the air.

NURSE. (*Hurries on with a glass of water.*) I was just getting him some aspirin and he gave me the slip.

(The CAST try again to proceed with the play.)

MRS. C. Rupert wants to leave Sarah.

EDWARD. Well before he does, perhaps he'd be kind enough to offer me a drink.

RUPERT. Help yourself.

NURSE. I have it here. (*Offers Edward the glass.*) Come along, drink it up.

EDWARD. What?

MRS. C. (*As before.*) This is Nurse Brown.

EDWARD. (*Lost again.*) Who?

MRS. C. Nurse Brown. She's just popped in.

EDWARD. I—I—(*Thoroughly bemused HE yells for a prompt.*) Yes! Prompt!

ANGELA. (*Off.*) Hang on. I've got a phone call to make.

EDWARD. (*Thinks this is his line.*) Hang on. I've got a phone call to make. (*HE starts to look for the telephone.*) Where is the bloody thing?

RUPERT. Who are you going to call? Kent, or Burgundy?

CHARLES. (*To Rupert.*) Oh for God's sake, shut up! (*Goes to Edward.*) Edward old man, we're not doing the play, the play's over.

EDWARD. Over?

CHARLES. Yes.

EDWARD. Ah. How did it go? My agent was out front.

SARAH. I'm sure he'll have been impressed.

EDWARD. He's young I'm afraid, far too young to have seen my performance in *King Lear.*

MRS. C. But he's heard about it.

EDWARD. Yes from me—ad nauseum, poor devil. But there's nothing to show for it. It's not on film or video, just a few dog-eared notices. Not much to show for a life's work in the theatre. What a tedious, pointless way of earning a living.

MRS. C. You've done some great work, Edward.

EDWARD. Not many great parts though.

MRS. C. Even in the smaller ones. Do you remember when we were together once in *Romeo and Juliet*?

EDWARD. (*Tries to focus his memory.*) No.

MRS. C. The Old Vic.

EDWARD. I remember The Old Vic, all right.

MRS. C. You were Friar Lawrence and I played the Nurse.

EDWARD. Oh yes—and lost.

(RUPERT laughs.)

MRS. C. I don't know why I bother to stick up for you.

EDWARD. Nor do I dear. Nor will my agent when he gets to know me better.

MADGE. I expect he'll be coming round to see you, I should go to your dressing room Edward.

EDWARD. Yes—I bought a bottle of champagne.

MRS. C. (*To the nurse.*) Would you see him upstairs?

NURSE. This way Mr. Frobisher.

EDWARD. (*As HE goes.*) If any of you feel like popping in for a snifter please do—I—I don't like drinking on my own.

MRS. C. You won't be on your own dear.

EDWARD. Don't bet on it.

(EDWARD and the NURSE exit.)

MRS. C. This profession has a lot to answer for.

CHARLES. No more than any other. Doctors, politicians, taxi- drivers, they can all go off the rails.

MRS. C. Yes, but with them it's the exception, with us it's the rule.

RUPERT. And you had the cheek to accuse me of being cynical.

MRS. C. The theatre's littered with disastrous marriages. I had one and Edward's had two.

RUPERT. That he can remember.

MRS. C. I wouldn't say yours was in a very healthy state.

RUPERT. It was fine until a rat started chewing into it.

MADGE. Don't kid yourself, I stopped loving you years ago.

RUPERT. Then I'm surprised you couldn't find an odd moment to mention the fact.

MADGE. I didn't want to hurt your feelings.

RUPERT. Ye Gods!!

MADGE. Stop playing to the gallery.

RUPERT. We haven't got a gallery.

MADGE. More trivia: Is it any wonder I grew tired of your boring, petty little jokes?

RUPERT. That's an overkill of adjectives darling. Petty or little, you don't need both.

MADGE. Unless of course you want to describe our marriage, because it's been both!

RUPERT. (*After a pause.*) I see—well—it was kind of you not to want to hurt my feelings.

CHARLES. I don't imagine there's anything I can say that will make you feel better.

RUPERT. Or worse, so don't flatter yourself.

CHARLES. I'm not just having an affair. (*Takes Madge's hand.*) I'm helplessly and totally in love with her.

RUPERT. I have the same problem.

CHARLES. Yes—well—we both understand how we feel.

RUPERT. You haven't the remotest idea how I feel, otherwise you wouldn't stand there making such bloody stupid remarks.

MADGE. *(To Rupert.)* Darling—I don't love you any more. I don't suppose it's the right time to tell you, but there it is.

RUPERT. And are you helplessly, totally in love with him?

MADGE. Yes I am. I'm sorry—but I am.

MRS. C. And if you still have any further murderous thoughts just curb them, we have another three months to run, and he's indispensable in the part of Charles.

RUPERT. He's got an understudy.

MRS. C. Not a particularly inspired one I'm afraid, so be a dear and don't rock the boat. I've just taken a mortgage out on a small cottage.

MADGE. Oh how lovely.

SARAH. Whereabouts?

MRS. C. Framfield.

CHARLES. Where's that?

MRS. C. Near Tunbridge Wells.

SARAH. Very nice, I've always wanted to live in Kent.

MRS. C. It's not quite as rural as it used to be, but there's a good train service and one has to think of these things at my age.

MADGE. I had an Aunt in Tunbridge Wells.

MRS. C. Very possibly. I think most Aunts end up there eventually.

CHARLES. You must've got a good price for your flat in Fulham.

MRS. C. It was certainly a great deal more than I paid for it, twenty years ago.

SARAH. I only rent my place.

CHARLES. Money down the drain darling.

MADGE. He's absolutely right.

CHARLES. In a precarious profession like ours, you've got to own bricks and mortar, it's the only way to save— believe me.

SARAH. Yes, that's what my accountant says.

CHARLES. Well listen to him. It's good advice (*To the others.*) wouldn't you agree?

MADGE. Definitely.

MRS. C. I can only speak from personal experience and—

RUPERT. (*Gives vent to a pent-up rage.*) Ah-h-h-h-!!

MRS. C. Don't you agree?

RUPERT. What the hell is everyone talking about?

MRS. C. There's no need to shout, we're not deaf.

RUPERT. I would've thought that if your wife tells you she's "helplessly and totally" in love with someone else, you're entitled to raise your voice by a decibel or two.

MADGE. You can raise it by twenty-two, but it won't alter what's happened. It's irreversible!

RUPERT. I don't agree. We might still manage to—

MADGE. Forget "we." It's not "we" any more—it's you and I.

RUPERT. (*Grabs her by the arms.*) Don't talk about it now. Not here, in front of all these goddam people.

MADGE. You brought the matter up in the first place.

CHARLES. And you threatened to kill me.

RUPERT. It wasn't a threat.

CHARLES. Oh good.

RUPERT. It was a promise.

CHARLES. Oh God.

EDWARD. (*Comes roaring back onto the stage, and heads towards Rupert.*) You bastard!

RUPERT. Now what's the matter?!

EDWARD. Bastard!

MRS. C. Do calm down, Edward—please.

EDWARD. That nurse has just told me of the havoc you have wrought tonight. I could kill you,

RUPERT. If you want to kill someone—kill him. (*Points to Charles.*) It's all his fault.

EDWARD. He didn't wreck the play and ruin my career.

RUPERT. I think there's an outside chance your career may survive this crisis, which is more than can be said for my marriage.

EDWARD. Who the hell cares about your marriage?

RUPERT. I do, for one.

EDWARD. Conceited oaf.

MADGE. Why don't you go back to the dressing room and wait for your agent?

EDWARD. He won't come now, not to see an old fool who forgets his lines, because his brain's addled in alcohol.

MRS. C. You mustn't talk about yourself like that.

EDWARD. Why not? Everyone else does.

CHARLES. That's not true.

EDWARD. Why do you think I left my previous agent? Because every time he put me up for a part he got the same answer—"Oh yes, Edward Frobisher, fine actor, good name to put above the title, but we've heard he's got a problem." Hardly surprising after fifty years of fighting to keep your foot on the bloody ladder—I had talent, lots of people get by without it, but at least I had it, or so I'm told, but what

I didn't have was something far more important, luck.
Twenty years ago I played Lear.
  RUPERT. And again tonight.
  EDWARD. (*Blankly.*) What?
  RUPERT. You gave us a couple of excerpts.
  EDWARD. Oh. (*A slight pause.*) How was I?
  MADGE. Marvellous.
  SARAH. Wonderful.
  EDWARD. It's not a big part, in fact it's the shortest
leading role in the entire Shakespeare Canon, but My God
you can strike sparks with it. (*HE launches forth again.*)
"Blow, winds, and crack your cheeks, rage, blow!"
  RUPERT. (*Aside.*) He's off again.
  EDWARD.
You cataracts and hurricanoes spout
Till you have drenched our steeples, drowned the cocks
You sulphurous and thought-executing fires
Vaunt-couriers to oak-cleaving thunderbolts
Singe my white head! And thou all shaking thunder
Smile flat the thick rotundity o'the world.
Crack nature's moulds, all germins spill at once.
That make ungrateful man!

(HE collapses dramatically.)

  RUPERT. What a ham. What a God-awful ham.
  MADGE. You don't know what you're saying.
  RUPERT. It's pitiful, and what's worse it's bad.
  MRS. C. Don't listen to him, Edward.
  RUPERT. Why shouldn't he? Why should he be fenced
off from reality? He's spent his whole life not listening, so

he's never heard the truth. He's not a great actor, he's a boring old fart.

MRS. C. Only a fool and a very vicious one could say such cruel things.

EDWARD. I didn't have the luck, laddie.

RUPERT. Balls: you had just as much luck as any of us, no more no less. What you didn't have was what Wolfit, Gielgud and Olivier had, and that's why they're remembered and you're not.

EDWARD. I can only assume that you're drunk.

RUPERT. Partly yes—but wholly honest.

MRS. C. If you were in the smallest degree talented yourself, one might excuse such a disgraceful outburst.

RUPERT. That's it, go on, defend him wrap him up in a nice cosy lie again.

EDWARD. (*Waves a hand weakly in Sarah's direction.*) Come and comfort your poor old father.

SARAH. (*Sits beside him.*) Are you all right?

EDWARD. I think I'm dying—dying. (*HE dozes off.*)

RUPERT. You see, he can't even be ill without acting it.

CHARLES. (*Vehemently.*) He has more talent in his little finger—

RUPERT. (*Cutting in.*) Yes—yes—yes. Don't you start. You're out of the same stable as he is. You can't wait to prance about in your jock-strap and tights.

CHARLES. You want to know something? You're eaten up with jealousy.

RUPERT. Jealousy?

CHARLES. You're no damn good as a classical actor. You haven't the qualities needed for Shakespeare so you despise him.

MADGE. I've never realized it before, but you're quite right. He does.

RUPERT. I'd be a raving idiot to despise the world's foremost playwright. What I find nauseating is the mantle of greatness an actor puts on when he plays in it. The intellectual aura he assumes, as if he'd written the bloody stuff. He gives interviews, on the radio—sounding like the Vice-Chancellor of Balliol.

EDWARD. What's he talking about?

SARAH. Playing in Shakespeare.

EDWARD. He's not going to do it, is he?

SARAH. No.

EDWARD. That'll be a relief to us all.

RUPERT. You think I couldn't?

EDWARD. I know you couldn't. Your acting's too thin, dear boy.

RUPERT. I get all the laughs.

EDWARD. We can all get laughs.

RUPERT. (*Points to Charles.*) He can't.

CHARLES. Bloody cheek.

MADGE. How dare you criticize him. He's a far better actor than you any day.

RUPERT. Love has obviously clouded your judgement. I shall accept nothing less than an unqualified apology for that last remark.

MADGE. Well you won't get it.

MRS. C. One must always be big enough to face the truth dear.

RUPERT. I take it you share my wife's jaundiced opinion?

MRS. C. Edward mentioned the value of luck in this business, and I'd say you'd had more than most of us.

RUPERT. I hope you won't be upset if you don't receive a Christmas card from me this year.

MRS. C. You mustn't take these things personally.

RUPERT. Oh thank you—I'll work at it.

CHARLES. (*Magnanimously.*) Any assessment of an actor's ability is bound to be subjective—I mean, one man's meat—

RUPERT. I refuse to accept any assessment of my talents from one of England's dreariest old character bags.

MRS. C. You beast!

(THEY rush to comfort her.)

MADGE. He didn't mean it.

MRS. C. Yes he did. (*In tears.*)

CHARLES. He's overwrought.

EDWARD. What's happened?

MRS. C. He said I was one of England's dreariest old character bags.

EDWARD. Oh I thought it was something serious. (*EDWARD dozes off again.*)

MRS. C. (*To Rupert.*) I shall never speak to you again.

RUPERT. You mustn't take these things personally.

MRS. C. In all my years in the theatre I have never been spoken to like that before.

RUPERT. Oh come on, you must've been.

MRS. C. Never!

MADGE. Don't listen to a word he's saying. He's just being thoroughly vindictive.

CHARLES. Probably due to drink.

RUPERT. Don't you kid yourself, when I'm drunk I can be downright rude.

MRS. C. I doubt if we'd notice the difference.

RUPERT. Look old darling, you started this slanging match, not me.

MRS. C. I happened to say you'd been lucky—and it's perfectly true. You have a facile comedy technique which works well enough on a good audience but there are many nights when I have to come on and pick the play up off the floor.

MADGE. (*Furious.*) When you what?

MRS. C. The stage is knee-deep in dropped laughs.

SARAH. You certainly can't blame that on me or Rupert.

RUPERT. Hear—hear.

MADGE. That's a very barbed remark if I may say so.

SARAH. It's a plain fact. You and Charles have all your good scenes in the second act so you just don't bother.

CHARLES. (*Angrily.*) You stupid girl. What the hell do you know about it?

RUPERT. Quite a lot, and she's got an award to prove it.

MADGE. I always felt it was totally unjustified.

SARAH. Well, you would wouldn't you?

CHARLES. If it wasn't for the fact that we feed you every line impeccably, I doubt if the critics would've even noticed you.

RUPERT. I've never heard such conceited twaddle: if she never opened her mouth at all, they'd notice her. She just has to walk on, stand, sit, or look out of a window. She has the gift of drawing the eye, the attention. It's called personality, an aura, or quite simply—magic.

MADGE. Are you sure she hasn't "doctored" your whisky?

RUPERT. I wouldn't expect you to agree—naturally.

CHARLES. Or me.

MADGE. She's lucky—that's all just lucky.

EDWARD. (*Coming to.*) What are they on about now?

MRS. C. Luck.

EDWARD. Ah—now, I have a theory about luck—would you—would you care to hear it?

RUPERT. Yes—tomorrow.

EDWARD. And tomorrow—and tomorrow—

RUPERT. And thank you and good night.

(EDWARD nods off again.)

MADGE. It's quite obvious my dear, that you're completely besotted with the girl.

RUPERT. And it's equally obvious that you're consumed with jealousy.

MADGE. For her? I wouldn't cast her in *Snow White*, except as one of the dwarfs.

RUPERT. By God, you're tough.

MADGE. I'll tell you what tough is. Tough is when you're nominated for a comedy award after twenty-five years in the business, years of hopes, disappointments and frustrations, and it goes to a younger woman with a vapid smile, reasonable legs, and a pair of firm breasts that do everything but wink!

CHARLES. But darling—you have all those things!!

RUPERT. Especially the vapid smile.

CHARLES. (*Hurriedly.*) I don't mean the smile.

MADGE. She's a tramp!

SARAH. No darling—you're the tramp.

RUPERT. I think she has a point.

MADGE. She worked on you—you idiot.

RUPERT. News to me.

MADGE. Oh come on—your eyes were out on stalks. You were eating out of her hand. "Can I get you some coffee?" "Would you like to sit here?" "I'll feed your meter for you." "What a pretty blouse—sweater—skirt—bottom."

RUPERT. Just a bloody moment. Let's remember who's been having it off with who shall we?

MADGE. A mere technicality, let's remember who stole who from who.

SARAH. I hope you're not accusing me.

MADGE. Who else?

SARAH. Until this evening, I swear I never held him in my arms.

MADGE. You didn't have to!

EDWARD. (*Roused.*) Devil of a lot of noise going on. I'm not "off" am I?

MRS. C. No, it's all right dear, our leading ladies are having a slight contretemps.

EDWARD. What's the cause?

MRS. C. Adultery.

EDWARD. (*Getting a cue from King Lear.*) Adultery?! Thou shall not die. Die for adultery! No.
(*Rising.*) The wren goes to't, and the small gilded fly
Does lecher in my sight.
Let copulation thrive!

MRS. C. It doesn't need any encouragement from you.

(*RUPERT gives her a little clap.*)

EDWARD. (*Turns to Sarah.*)
Behold yon simpering dame,
Whose face between her forks presages snow,
That minces virtue and does shake the head
To hear of pleasure's name.
The fitchew, nor the spoiled horse, goes to't
With a more riotous appetite.

(*Then indicating Sarah and Madge.*)

Down from the waist they are centaurs
Though women all above:
But to the girdle do the Gods inherit,
Beneath is all the fiends
There's hell, there's darkness, there's the sulphorous pit.
Burning, scalding, stench, consumption. Fie, fie, fie, pah!
Pah! Give me an ounce of civet, good Apothecary, to
sweeten my imagination. There's money for thee.
    RUPERT. There's a couple of quid for thee too.
(*Pretends to give him a tip.*) Very good. I enjoyed that. I
must give old Shakespeare another go one day. He certainly
doesn't mince matters.
    EDWARD. My head's spinning.
    CHARLES. Sit down, old man.
    EDWARD. There's the last act to do yet.
    CHARLES. Don't worry.

(*EDWARD is helped onto the sofa.*)

    EDWARD. Must keep on top—got my agent in.
    MRS. C. It's going beautifully.

CHARLES. My God, what a talent. It's a privilege. to have been on this stage tonight—moments like that are so rare—so very rare.

RUPERT. I'm glad I spared you then.

CHARLES. No, seriously, I doubt if there's been anything as electrifying as that since the days of Max Reinhardt.

RUPERT. Or even Max Miller.

CHARLES. You really are an ignorant crud aren't you?

RUPERT. A quotation from the Bard no doubt.

MADGE. I wouldn't waste your breath on him. He's a destroyer. Anything he doesn't understand he kills off—love, emotion, art, marriage.

RUPERT. OK. OK. But could you just switch your bloody mouth off for a second.

MADGE. I do hope you improve your manners when you shack up with your child-bride, if she'll have you.

MRS. C. And doesn't mind living with a third-rate Repertory actor,

RUPERT. I'd say that was veering towards the venomous, wouldn't you?

CHARLES. No more than you deserve.

RUPERT. I can't think why I ever risked my freedom to deprive you of yours.

CHARLES. I'm surprised you didn't though, being a right little show-off, bent on cheap theatricality.

MRS. C. Just like his acting.

MADGE. (*Eyeing Sarah.*) And her's.

MRS. C. I sometimes wonder if these Awards aren't fixed.

RUPERT. It's quite obvious you've never won any.

MRS. C. (*Flaring up.*) I'm not bitter about it.

RUPERT. No, no, just mildly surprised.

MRS. C. I blame television, nobody knows how to project anymore. They mumble in front of a microphone and call it acting. They don't even have to have a thought in their head, the camera does it all for them.

RUPERT. I suppose you feel we should all go leaping and lurching about like Edward.

MRS. C. You couldn't hold a candle to him.

RUPERT. I wouldn't even try—he'd ignite.

CHARLES. She's absolutely right about your performance at the beginning of the play.

RUPERT. I beg your pardon?

CHARLES. Well—I mean—I'm not trying to tell you how to play the part.

RUPERT. No of course not—but you will.

CHARLES. No, that would be pompous in the extreme, but there is a sort—a sort of "holding back" in your general approach I feel.

RUPERT. (*Pause.*) My general approach?

CHARLES. (*Pause.*) Yes.

RUPERT. Would you care to be more specific?

CHARLES. (*Faltering.*) Well I mean, obviously one's opinion has got to be subjective of course.

RUPERT. (*Holding himself in check.*) Of course.

CHARLES. And it's very difficult to be specific, but for instance when you make your first entrance—

RUPERT. That seems fairly specific.

CHARLES. Well I didn't mean to be—but you did ask.

RUPERT. I did indeed. I'm all ears.

CHARLES. Rupert's marriage has blown up in his face after fifteen years, it's a pretty devastating moment, and you come on as if you are packing a bag to go off on a golfing week-end.

RUPERT. (*Pause.*) I see.

CHARLES. (*Looking around for support.*) I mean, that's just my own opinion I can't speak for anyone else.

MRS. C. My dear boy, I'm so glad you've said it. You've hit the nail on the head.

RUPERT. (*Inwardly seething.*) It's an interesting thought.

CHARLES. I'm not saying it's your fault entirely.

RUPERT. Oh—aren't you?

CHARLES. Well clearly the director must take some of the responsibility.

RUPERT. Ah.

CHARLES. But he's probably been taken in, to a degree, by your style of acting.

RUPERT. Which is?

CHARLES. Well—er—shall we say, understatement?

MRS. C. Or underacting.

RUPERT. OK. Let's start again.

CHARLES. Sorry?

RUPERT. From my first entrance.

MADGE. Darling, don't be a fool.

RUPERT. No no. Fair do's. He could be right. It's an interesting theory. Just get into your positions roughly and I'll try it another way.

MRS. C. (*Rising.*) Edward and I aren't on when you enter.

RUPERT. Doesn't matter, stay where you are. I'd like you to give me a few pointers. (*HE goes to exit.*) Just give me two or three lines up to my entrance.

SARAH. I exit just before you come on.

RUPERT. Right go from there.
MADGE. Don't forget the trunk.
RUPERT. What?
MADGE. You bring the trunk on.
RUPERT. Oh yes. (*RUPERT takes the trunk off.*
THEY now revert to the play.)
SARAH. Are you ready?
RUPERT. (*Off.*) Yes.
SARAH. Have you finished with the apple amber?
CHARLES. Yes, thank you.
MADGE. It was delicious Sarah.

(*SARAH picks up an imaginary plate and exits to the
kitchen.*)

CHARLES. Not quite as good as yours darling.
MADGE. I shouldn't mention the fact.
CHARLES. 'Course not.

(*RUPERT enters with the trunk and he does the full
HENRY IRVING.*)

RUPERT. My God!! (*HE drops the trunk.*) Are you
still here?!
CHARLES. Sorry old man.
RUPERT. No! It's all right. (*Gives a maniacal laugh.*)
Just as well really. I've got a little tidying up to do. You'll
be able to calm her down when I'm gone. (*Another crazy
laugh and staggers.*)
CHARLES. She seems reasonably calm at the moment.
RUPERT. Before the next storm.
MADGE. I can't tell you how sorry we are Rupert.

RUPERT. (*Leaps around.*) Oh, can't you?

CHARLES. (*Nervously.*) And if there's anything we can do—

RUPERT. *(Doing a "Lear.")* Well there isn't is there? We've run aground. Hit the rocks! It's a total wreck. (*Sobs.*) Nothing to salvage!!

CHARLES. (*By now totally embarrassed.*) I'm not sure what sparked the whole thing off. (*Comes out of the play.*) This is bloody ridiculous.

RUPERT. (*Picks up the knife.*) Get on with it.

CHARLES. (*Reverts to the play.*) I mean there we were, thoroughly enjoying the pork en croute, and the next minute the balloon had gone up.

RUPERT. (*Going into Olivier's Richard III.*) We got married that's what started it.

MADGE. But—that was twenty years ago.

RUPERT. And that outburst tonight has finished it. My only regret is that two of our dearest friends should have been here to witness it. But one can't legislate for the volcanic eruptions of life!!

SARAH. (*Enters.*) I'm stacking the machine so if— (*SHE stops on seeing Rupert and then pulls all the stops out to match Rupert's performance.*) For Christ's sake— don't tell me you're staying?

RUPERT. (*Hunched and limping over to her.*) I wouldn't stay if I had two broken legs and a heart attack.

SARAH. What are you doing—writing me a farewell note?

RUPERT. I'm just getting my personal effects. (*Puts his hands round her throat.*) If you've no objection!

SARAH. (*Half throttled.*) We're dividing the property already are we? What are you taking—the sofa?

RUPERT. (*Darts to desk.*) Credit cards, check book, that's all.

SARAH. (*Clutching her throat dramatically.*) Not—not the joint one?

RUPERT. (*Cackles.*) Well I can't see it makes much difference.

SARAH. (*Grabs the knife.*) Put the bloody thing back!!

RUPERT. (*Cowering.*) All right, all right.

SARAH. You see what he's like—devious.

RUPERT. The account's empty anyway.

SARAH. And mean.

RUPERT. (*Leaps at her.*) Who spent it all?

SARAH. (*Standing her ground.*) In case you've been away, some shops now make a small charge for food, wine, brandy, cigars.

RUPERT. Oh that rapier wit. In future all communication will be carried out through my solicitor.

CHARLES. (*Flatly.*) Just a minute, that's me.

RUPERT. Oh God!!So it is!!

MADGE. That'll make things awfully awkward. (*Comes out of the play.*) All right, you've made your point—now—

RUPERT. (*Threatens her with the knife.*) Give me the next line!!

MADGE. (*Reverts to the play.*) Why don't you just separate?

SARAH. We don't want to separate.

RUPERT. No, it's got to be divorce, for the sake of the children.

CHARLES. You haven't got any children!

RUPERT. Not by Sarah, but with my next wife the place will be crawling with them.

SARAH. Someone in mind have you?

RUPERT. Plenty. (*A loud cackle.*)

SARAH. Oh it's a harem is it? Now Look Charles. (*Bearing down on him.*)

CHARLES. (*Coming out of the play.*) Can we stop now?

(*EDWARD has woken up and is confused.*)

SARAH. (*Grips Charles's throat.*) Now look Charles, you're our solicitor not his, so you can represent me. O.K.?

CHARLES. Well—

RUPERT. Balls—Charles was my friend long before you came on the scene.

EDWARD. Where the hell are we now?

MRS. C. Act One, dear.

EDWARD. Sod it, I'm in the wrong act!! (*HE attempts to get up.*)

MRS. C. It's all right.

EDWARD. But my agent—

MRS. C. He understands what's happened.

EDWARD. That's more than I do.

RUPERT. (*Hamming it up.*) We were up at Oxford together. It's been a lifelong association.

EDWARD. (*Rising.*) Don't you mock me, boy!

RUPERT. Siddown.

EDWARD. He's stolen all my inflections.

SARAH. (*Still in the play.*) There you are, that's all he thinks of—money—money—money—

EDWARD. Sod the money—it's my bloody inflections.

MRS. C. Edward dear, please sit down.

RUPERT. (*Still in the play.*) It won't be too far from your mind when you're trying to live on your allowance.

SARAH. I doubt if I shall notice the difference.

EDWARD. She's as bad as he is.

MADGE. Actually Charles isn't a specialist in divorce.

CHARLES. More conveyancing really.

EDWARD. Certainly not acting. (*To Rupert.*) And as for you—you're all over the bloody shop. Take it calmly— "We were up at Oxford together. It's been a lifelong association." It's supposed to be conversational, not Henry the fucking Fifth.

NURSE. (*Enters.*) You'll be pleased to hear I've managed to get hold of a doctor, for Mr. Frobisher.

MRS. C. What a relief.

EDWARD. Who are you?

NURSE. The Nurse.

EDWARD. The Nurse?

NURSE. (*Takes him by the arm.*) Come along now.

EDWARD. Why should I?

NURSE. (*Tactfully.*) You're in the wrong act. You're drunk.

EDWARD. You think I'm drunk? You're in the wrong bloody play!

SARAH. (*Pressing on.*) Who wants coffee?

RUPERT. I wouldn't mind some.

EDWARD. (*Wrenching himself free.*) Nor would I. (*To Rupert.*) But first of all get the damn speech right. "We were up at Oxford together. It's been a lifelong association."

RUPERT. (*Mimicking Edward's "King Lear."*) "We were up at Oxford together. It's been a lifelong association."

EDWARD. (*Seething.*) I'll kill him. I'll kill him.

CHARLES. Not worth it, old boy.

NURSE. Gently now. (*The NURSE tries to restrain him.*)

EDWARD. Leave me alone thou Midnight hag! This jackinapes is making a fool of me.

RUPERT. My impersonation must've been better than I realized.

CHARLES. Don't fool yourself.

MADGE. It was mean and cruel.

RUPERT. (*With a mocking bow.*) Thank you for your kind appreciation.

CHARLES. That hammy performance was only fractionally better than your straight one.

RUPERT. By God, you've had it now. (*RUPERT grabs Charles by the throat.*)

CHARLES. Get him off!!

(*As MADGE and MRS. CULLEN attempt to pull RUPERT back, ANGELA rushes on.*)

ANGELA. (*Shouts up to the flies.*) Go curtain!

VOICE. (*From the flies.*) I haven't had the cue!

ANGELA. It's a new ending! Bring it down!

(*The CURTAIN descends with MADGE, SARAH and MRS. CULLEN trying to separate the two men and the NURSE attempting to take EDWARD off against his will. The CURTAIN rises again as if it was a normal*

performance. The audience APPLAUSE catches the CAST somewhat by surprise and through force of habit THEY stop what they are doing and saying, and ALL take their bows wherever they happen to be.
The CURTAIN descends again and then rises. The CAST have resumed their struggle but once again stop to acknowledge the APPLAUSE and this time ANGELA and the NURSE also feel obliged to bow.)

EDWARD. (*Suddenly notices Angela and the nurse bowing.*) What the hell are you bowing for? You're not in it!! Bloody amateurs!

THE CURTAIN FINALLY DESCENDS

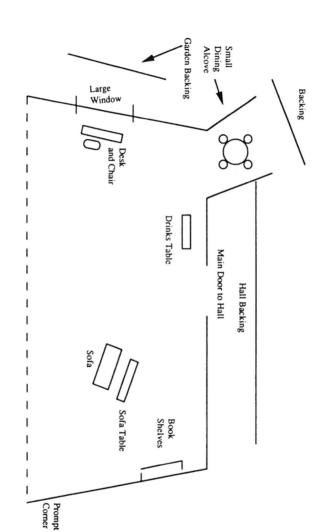

Kindly Leave the Stage

SKIN DEEP
Jon Lonoff

Comedy / 2m, 2f / Interior Unit Set

In *Skin Deep*, a large, lovable, lonely-heart, named Maureen Mulligan, gives romance one last shot on a blind-date with sweet awkward Joseph Spinelli; she's learned to pepper her speech with jokes to hide insecurities about her weight and appearance, while he's almost dangerously forthright, saying everything that comes to his mind. They both know they're perfect for each other, and in time they come to admit it.

They were set up on the date by Maureen's sister Sheila and her husband Squire, who are having problems of their own: Sheila undergoes a non-stop series of cosmetic surgeries to hang onto the attractive and much-desired Squire, who may or may not have long ago held designs on Maureen, who introduced him to Sheila. With Maureen particularly vulnerable to both hurting and being hurt, the time is ripe for all these unspoken issues to bubble to the surface.

"Warm-hearted comedy … the laughter was literally show-stopping. A winning play, with enough good-humored laughs and sentiment to keep you smiling from beginning to end."
- TalkinBroadway.com

"It's a little Paddy Chayefsky, a lot Neil Simon and a quick-witted, intelligent voyage into the not-so-tranquil seas of middle-aged love and dating. The dialogue is crackling and hilarious; the plot simple but well-turned; the characters endearing and quirky; and lurking beneath the merriment is so much heartache that you'll stand up and cheer when the unlikely couple makes it to the inevitable final clinch."
- NYTheatreWorld.Com

COCKEYED
William Missouri Downs

Comedy / 3m, 1f / Unit Set

Phil, an average nice guy, is madly in love with the beautiful Sophia. The only problem is that she's unaware of his existence. He tries to introduce himself but she looks right through him. When Phil discovers Sophia has a glass eye, he thinks that might be the problem, but soon realizes that she really can't see him. Perhaps he is caught in a philosophical hyperspace or dualistic reality or perhaps beautiful women are just unaware of nice guys. Armed only with a B.A. in philosophy, Phil sets out to prove his existence and win Sophia's heart. This fast moving farce is the winner of the HotCity Theatre's GreenHouse New Play Festival. The St. Louis Post-Dispatch called Cockeyed a clever romantic comedy, Talkin' Broadway called it "hilarious," while Playback Magazine said that it was "fresh and invigorating."

Winner!
of the HotCity Theatre GreenHouse New Play Festival

"Rocking with laughter...hilarious...polished and engaging work draws heavily on the age-old conventions of farce: improbable situations, exaggerated characters, amazing coincidences, absurd misunderstandings, people hiding in closets and barely missing each other as they run in and out of doors...full of comic momentum as Cockeyed hurtles toward its conclusion."
- Talkin' Broadway

CPSIA information can be obtained at www.ICGtesting.com
Printed in the USA
BVOW011420150413

318226BV00009B/148/P